The Goetist

Warren Tusk

APOCRYPHILE
PRESS

Apocryphile Press
PO Box 255
Hannacroix, NY 12087
www.apocryphilepress.com

Copyright © 2026 by Warren Tusk
Printed in the United States of America
ISBN 978-1-965646-31-1 | paper
ISBN 978-1-965646-32-8 | ePub

No part of this book may be reproduced, stored in a retrieval system, or transmitted in any form or by any means—electronic, mechanical, photocopy, recording, or otherwise—without written permission of the author and publisher, except for brief quotations in printed reviews.

Please join our mailing list at www.apocryphilepress.com/free. We'll keep you up-to-date on all our new releases, and we'll also send you a FREE BOOK. Visit us today!

Contents

1. The Summoning — 1
2. Magic — 6
3. Desire — 8
4. Necessity — 11
5. Joy — 13
6. Reality — 15
7. The Soul — 18
8. Morality — 21
9. Solitude — 24
10. Fellowship — 27
11. Dominion — 30
12. Myth — 33
13. Symbolism — 36
14. The World — 39
15. Civilization — 42
16. Government — 44
17. Constraint — 48
18. Choice — 51
19. Art — 54
20. Vice — 56
21. Hatred — 58
22. Greatness — 61
23. Immortality — 64
24. Legacy — 67
25. Perfection — 70
26. Failure — 72
27. Hope — 76
28. The Banishing — 80

The Summoning

In my thirty-fifth year, I lost my faith in all the wisdom that I had learned, and in those who had taught me.

My time stretched out before me like a corridor, long and close, dusty and shabby.

And there were words written upon the walls of that corridor, but they were not my own. They were signs and slogans and advertisements, and I was humiliated to look upon them.

And though I could turn to the left or to the right, into adjoining hallways—I knew well that it would be no different to walk those halls, and that they would lead me to the same end.

So it was that I sat alone upon a train platform, and grieved for the days of my life, which I had tossed away like beads of colored glass.

I looked upon the water, and upon the lights that danced on the water, and upon the lights of the city on the far shore, and upon the lights of the train that approached from the dusk. And my

The Goetist

heart cried out like a hungry babe, yearning to encompass the loveliness that I saw, aching for a balm unto my melancholy.

I wished for a life that could be filled with the feelings of beauty and joy.

Then I was ashamed. My mind was wiser than my heart; I knew well enough not to chase after *feelings*. Mere feelings cannot heal the wounds of the spirit. But in my heart I was foolish, and like a child. When I felt bad, I wanted nothing more than to feel good.

The thing I needed was an unnameable quality of existence, the quality evoked by lights in the gloam. Whatever feelings would come from a life marked by that quality, they would be worth the feeling.

But I did not understand, and I knew not what to do, except to sit on the train platform and stare out.

I thought upon the guides and counselors who had brought me to that point, and I spat.

I thought upon my friends, whom I loved, who would surely be kind to me. But they could tell me nothing that I needed to hear.

Then did I vow to seek wisdom from those who were older and greater than I—from those far-seeing intellects who had known the radiant heights and the terrible depths.

In the marketplace, I purchased all that I would need: a robe of good white linen, and a sharp sword, and fine perfumes, and parchment, and ink, and materials for an offering.

And I betook myself to the house of my father, for in that house were kept the lore-books of elder days. It stood far from the press

The Summoning

of the city, and there I could do what I needed to do, without trouble or disturbance.

From ragged, dusty paper I learned how to begin.

In the basement of that house I prepared the rite. In the cool and the dark and the quiet, it was done. Upon the ground I chalked all the figures, and the words from the scriptures.

Then I dressed myself in that linen robe, and anointed myself with those perfumes. In my hands I held the sword, and the talisman that I had inked upon the parchment; and I stood in the very center of the circle that I had drawn, behind words, behind words, behind words. And there did I utter the invocation that I had learned.

When I finished, and the universe did not tremble, I uttered it again. Over and over I recited the spell, until my brain burned within my skull, until every word through my throat was salt in a wound. I did not stop, because I did not know what I would do if I stopped.

I do not know how long I spoke. I know only that it was long enough.

For it came to pass that the air in that basement grew thick and sulfurous, and the light in my eyes became strange. The fire in the brazier leapt and danced.

A demon appeared before me, in the triangle of chalk that I had prepared for him.

He was dressed in a black coat, with a broad black hat upon his head. His face lay hidden in darkness, but in his eyes there glowed the radiance of Hell. He carried an iron lantern, which cast strange shadows upon the walls.

In that moment I put the authority of a magician into my voice, and I said, I have conjured you, demon, and bound you. Now you stand here, within my power. Now you answer to my will. Now you will do as I command.

The demon smiled at me then. There was no anger in his face, nor fear, only a mocking pity; and in that moment I could not believe myself his master, and I knew dread.

But his voice was gentle as he answered, saying:

What would you have of me, O magus? Shall I fetch for you the treasures of the earth? Shall I gift you with the power of fire and storm? Shall I bring torment to your foes, or longing to your beloved?

And I replied, No, none of those. I have not called you here for trinkets.

From you I would have the understanding that you have won through all your aeons of learning and watching and damnation.

From you I would learn the way of living well.

He laughed at that. And his smile was broad as he answered, saying:

Wisdom is born from scope of vision.

The first lesson is that many things are impossible in a human life; for man is not infinitely plastic, and if he seeks to twist himself into a shape that he cannot hold, he will break.

The Summoning

The second lesson is that many more things are possible in a human life than can be seen with mortal eyes; for it is the way of men to blind each other, and themselves.

These lessons having been taught—

—what ignorance troubles the currents of your soul, O mortal man?

Magic

Then did I command the demon,
Speak to me of magic.
And the demon answered, saying:

The magician's art is unlike any natural or worldly thing.

Children and dreamers yearn for magic, but they know not the nature of their yearning. Their imagination does not encompass the truth of their desire. What they name *magic* in their minds is not magic, and cannot satisfy the hunger of their souls.

Judge not magic by its power, for there is power great and terrible in the arts of the un-enchanted world. Judge not magic by its mystery, for the un-enchanted world contains wonders that have never yet been apprehended by man.

Magic is the lantern that shines upon your mind and your spirit, and casts their shadows into reality.

Magic is the power of innocence, which can be wielded only by the pure of heart—and the power of corruption, which can be

Magic

wielded only by the wicked—and every other power that takes its shape from the shape of thought.

Magic is the god-monster that eats the sacrifices offered unto it, and gives its blessings in proportion to the horror of the sacrifice.

Magic is the thing that cannot be cheated, and does not cheat.

Magic is the thing that sees, and cares, in a blind uncaring universe.

The scientist wields power because he knows the world; but the magician wields power because he knows himself.

This is the yearning of the child, and of the dreamer—that there should be power found within the truth of their own souls, and that when they stand alone and ignorant in the teeth of the universe, their power will not abandon them.

But all this you knew already, for it is by magic that you have conjured me here.

Desire

Then did I command the demon,
Speak to me of desire.
And the demon answered, saying:

You have heard the master tell you that suffering is born of desire. And this is so. But I will tell you a greater truth: that desire is born of suffering.

The child in the womb has all that he needs. He can conceive of nothing that he does not already have. He does not hurt, he does not yearn, and he is contented.

When an infant is born, he enters into a world filled with treasures that he does not possess. Some, he craves instinctively—food, rest, cleanness, love. Some he learns to crave by imitating the people around him. Some he comes to crave only as he begins to exercise his imagination. He hears, or reads, stories of the unreal; unreal beauties are thrust upon him; and so he is taught to cast covetous eyes upon unreal dreams. Thus does he cease to be a beast, and grow into humanity.

Desire

In wanting, and not having, he discovers what it is to feel pains of the heart.

There is more joy in desire than in the fulfillment of desire. A thing, attained, can be only itself. But the imagining of a thing, the expectation of a thing, can be every pleasure and every fulfillment of the soul. If you want it, and it is beyond your grasp, then your imagined delight in it can be infinite. And that imagining need never end, until the desire is fulfilled, or you lose hope. If you wish to be happy, then take pains to see that you are never quite satisfied, and keep your vision always upon the next object of your greed.

(In this way, you may discover that happiness is not truly what you crave.)

All thought is born from desire. The mind is a devisor of stratagems to obtain what you want and do not have. Every action, and every contemplation, is an attempt to bridge the gap between longing and satisfaction. If you hope for contentment, it is a hope for a return to the womb. Which is to say, a hope for oblivion.

So it is that desire is the first shaper of the self. When you look upon yourself consciously, you will see a creature that hungers for things. All your traits and attributes, all your skills and powers, are tools crafted to feed the hunger. If you are to love yourself, then you must love the hungering. If you are to value your own existence, then you must find goodness in the fact of the hungering—more goodness than you would find in satiety.

This is the ordinary way of things, for men. They fear nothing so much as the perfect fulfillment of their desires, which would render their souls as naught.

When men fight over their ideals, or their imagined utopias, in truth they are fighting only over their divergent conceptions of desire. *Which yearnings are base, and should be satisfied expediently, so that we need struggle with them no longer? Which yearnings are noble, and should be left unsatisfied in perpetuity, so that they may continue to define us?*

Nothing soothes the heart so well as a thing for which you can yearn, and ache, and tremble, *even as you possess it.* This is called love.

Necessity

Then did I command the demon,
Speak to me of necessity.
And the demon answered, saying:

Necessity is the iron chain that binds.

Every man who needs what he does not have is a slave; for the world may command him, and punish him for his disobediences.

A beast, suffocating, can think of nothing but air. A beast, starving, can think of nothing but food. Only with the fulfillment of his needs can a man become more than a beast. Only when he has what he needs can he learn what he desires. Only then can he learn who he is.

If you conquer your need, it will plague you no more. If you slake your need, it will return to you, again and again. But the conquest of need is a long road, and a hard one; and if you give great swathes of your life and your mind to the work, then you may lose more than you gain.

The Goetist

A man who has what he needs may yearn to chase after it nonetheless. He may dream fondly of seeking water in the desert, or of tilling the soil to alleviate his hunger pangs; he may dream of being lonely, and finding love to ease his heart. This is the nostalgia that a free man feels for his days of slavery. It is the urge to walk away from a difficult, frightening quest to walk a simpler road. And if you wish to be a slave, and to know simplicity, then by all means deny yourself the fulfillment of your needs—but know that you are your only master, and that the hand holding the whip is your own.

If you would be a liberator unto others, and raise them from the station of beasts, then give them what they need. But do not expect for this their gratitude, or their service. No one has less capacity to bend than the man who has just come into his own desires, and been freed from the shackles of necessity.

A man may yearn to be needed by his family, or his fellows. Thus would he enslave them, and hold their well-being hostage to his own importance.

Be an ornament for those whom you cherish, and not a yoke.

JOY

Then did I command the demon,
Speak to me of joy.
And the demon answered, saying:

Joy is the bait in the snare,
    and the nectar upon the leaf of the pitcher plant;
Joy is the sacred deer, which must not be hunted.

You have heard it rightly said, that a man can know joy for no longer than a single moment, before it departs in its caprice. Even for a sage, in all his enlightenment, it will not stay for longer than two. And the man who seeks to grasp joy, and hold it close, will find that he has only chased it beyond the precincts of his life.

For the human heart was not meant to dwell in lasting bliss. Happiness is a reward, given by your unconscious mind unto your conscious mind, for the attainment of the most precious and useful things; and it is doled out very sparingly, that you may hunger for it always, and in its name pursue every valuable opportunity.

But your unconscious mind does not know the needs of your spirit. If you bite at its bait and do its bidding, you will spend all your days running after illusions, and snatching ever at a joy that eludes you, and attaining nothing of true worth.

What, then, is the course of wisdom? For a man cannot excise from himself the desire to feel joy, any more than he can swallow his own head. And should he endeavor to put that desire aside, in his misery he will only crave it all the more.

There is only one path forward, which is—to walk another path.

Look beyond your joy, and fix your eyes upon a thing that you love. It may be that you love that thing because it brings you joy. So be it; but look to the thing itself, and not to the state of your heart. Value what you love, for its own sake. Serve it well, with all your might and all your vision. Let your emotions fall away from the enterprise.

In attending to the object of your adoration, you will find peace. Perhaps, from time to time, you may even find joy.

If the object of your adoration is the shape of your own soul—if you are determined to exalt yourself, and not to be dissuaded by the fluxions of happiness and sorrow—then you may have the makings of a worthy magician.

Reality

Then did I command the demon,
Speak to me of reality.
And the demon answered, saying:

The material world around you—made of particles and energy—that is reality. And if you ignore it, or deny its power, then it will destroy you.

The world of abstractions—made of imaginings and possibilities—that, also, is reality. And it too will destroy you, if you do not recognize it for what it is.

Every pattern is real. And every story and symbol, every myth and fantasy, every idea and belief, is a pattern. These things are *information*; they can be expressed in ones and zeroes, given a long enough tape on which to write them, and a perfect divine lexicon. You have seen for yourself that information exists, even beyond the particular material substances in which it is expressed.

As men thrive, and grow in enlightenment, their minds move slowly from the material realm to the realm of abstraction.

In the mind of the man who cannot breathe, nothing is real, except for air.

In the mind of the man who is burning alive, nothing is real, except the necessity of saving his physical flesh from the physical fire. And if he can think upon a Heaven beyond the dust of the earth, even in that moment, then he is a saint.

The mind of the man without food is focused mostly on eating. The mind of the man without a home is focused mostly on sheltering himself from the elements. The mind of the lonely man is focused mostly on companionship. And if he can think upon abstractions and immaterial imaginings, even under such circumstances, then his mind is deep and profound; or else he is clutching them to his heart for succor, and not thinking upon them at all.

But in the mind of the man who is well-provisioned and well-beloved—

—the material world falls away, and immaterial concerns fill the whole of creation.

Titles and dignities, laws and borders—these things have less weight than air, and yet men kneel before them, and kill in their name. They tear out their hearts over thoughts of thoughts of thoughts, even if none of it is ever communicated to anyone, not even in a single word. The love and the courage of fictional people, who never stepped once upon the earth, have force enough to define the lives of people made from flesh and bone.

Humans are material creatures, and they can never entirely escape the world of the material, not so long as they live. A sage is a few days of starvation away from being a beast; and even the most abstracted philosopher has a meat-brain that thinks in terms of its perceptions and its sensations, from which he cannot escape no matter what he believes.

But through the alchemy of thought, those perceptions and sensations can be transmuted into the most fantastical patterns of imagination. And it is within the imagination that the highest glories may be achieved.

Understanding the nature of reality is the beginning of wisdom.

Wielding power over the immaterial
    is the essence of the magician's art.

The Soul

*Then did I command the demon,
Speak to me of the soul.
And the demon answered, saying:*

The servants of God have forgotten the nature of the soul, which once they knew.

Your soul is not a homunculus in your head, ruling and piloting your body. It is not the secret ethereal seat of your intelligence. It is not a vital fluid, or a mysterious vapor, or any thing that could be extracted and put in a jar. It does not fly away from your material form upon your death, to continue being you in some other plane of existence.

As the philosopher said, it is nothing more or less than this: the essential form of the creature that you are.

Your soul is the very fact of your self, perceived in its totality. It is the concatenation of all the attributes and abstractions and occurrences that define you, and of all their interactions with one another. It is the complete truth of what you are, the incorruptible cosmic record of your existence. It is the information within which you are recorded.

So long as you are mortal and material, your soul cannot be separated from your body, any more than you can be separated from your own height.

But, by the same token, it is plain how a human might dare to dream of a spiritual immortality. The accident of your matter will disintegrate, but your essential form can and must exist forever, even as the very stars fade and perish.

The exhortation of every divine discipline is this: *Care not for the perspective of your mortal shell, which is a thing of happenstance, but place your heart and your hope in the very fact of your soul. All that you think and all that you do, in every moment, gives shape to that soul, which is eternal.* And this, too, is the exhortation of the demons. The difference lies only in the shapes that you might seek to take, and in the governance that you choose to accept with regard to the shaping.

Every thing that is, and indeed every thing that is not, has a soul. There is a perfect formal abstraction of every possible entity, real and unreal. Remember, then, the ensoulment of every thing that you destroy. For destruction is essential to existence. A human being cannot go an hour, nay, not even a minute, without annihilating something whose form will perdure eternally in Heaven or in Hell.

But the human mind is built to perceive patterns as stories; and those patterns that do not make stories are often incomprehensible, and almost always meaningless. What do you care for the infinitely complex attributes that define a single rock? Or a particular bowl's worth of air? Or a specific curve along the surface of the moon?

A human may live by any code that he pleases, and call it morality. But if you would understand the hidden ethics that underlie human actions, behind their conscious thoughts and ideals, then you must know this: *If an entity's existence does not constitute a narrative, then it has no soul worth consideration, and there is no moral weight to its existence.*

Humans differ in the kinds of stories that they have learned to perceive.

Men move forward in time, and not backward; and so it is that, from a human perspective, the soul of an entity can become more real but never less so. An attribute, once you acquire it, will always serve to define you. Even if it ceases to be real in the present, it will forever have been real in the past. Your soul will forever be the soul of someone *for whom that thing was true*, and this gives you texture and meaning, just as the life of a man in a storybook has meaning even after you read of his fictional death. But the future is unknown, and moreover, it is malleable. A trait that you do not yet possess is nothing, and a moral man can discard it without a qualm.

Morality

Then did I command the demon,
Speak to me of morality.
And the demon answered, saying:

Morality is a story that you tell yourself, of the shape that you wish for the world to take.

Though you sift through all the sands of every desert on every planet, you will not find one particle of good, nor a single shred of evil. Though you strain all the waters of the universe through a sieve, you will find no justice and no holiness. Good and evil, justice and holiness, are things of story; they exist in our minds, and not in the world.

Though you devote yourself to wisdom and right conduct, the vicissitudes of human life will never be encompassed by your doctrines, whatsoever they may be. And countless men who embrace wickedness, in your eyes, will show themselves to be wise and joyful and noble and kind; and countless men who cling to righteousness will show themselves to be vicious and miserable and vapid and petty.

(And if you turned your face against wisdom, or joy, or nobility, or kindness—if you saw fit to exalt viciousness, or misery, or vapidity, or pettiness, as the path of the right—who could prove that you had the wrong of it?)

There are those who say, Good and evil surely exist in the world; for all men know, in their deepest hearts, what is good and what is evil. They know nothing of their fellow men, and they have no imagination besides. For the human heart can take as many shapes as there are stars in the sky. What one man finds beautiful, and noble, is repulsive unto another. This is so, even unto the heights of virtue and the depths of wickedness. And even if it were otherwise: all men may believe a thing, and yet be deluded.

There are those who say, Good and evil *must* exist in the world, for otherwise we could not bear it. They are cowards, and children. There are many truths that men cannot bear.

There are those who say, Morality does not exist in the world, and so it is nothing, and less than nothing; and good and evil are illusions, with no power to bind; and every thing is as worthy as every other, and a man has no reason to abide by any code.

To them I can only say, If you love yourself so little, and there is so little value in the stories that you tell—better for you that you had never been born.

The wise man will bind his thoughts and his deeds into the shape that he wishes for them to take, and keep them bound even as the binding grows painful. For without it he would have no shape at all. And without it, if he contemplated the purpose of his existence, he would find nothing.

The courageous man is prepared to kill, and to die, in the name of the ideals that he invented himself. And he strives with all his might to subordinate all the world to his vision, if he can. For is it not the worthiest of visions? Were it not so—would he not have invented something different?

And all this, too, is moralizing.

You have heard the philosophers say, The worth of a deed is measured by what comes of it—or, The worth of a deed is measured by the virtues upon which it draws—or, The worth of a deed is measured by the Law, when the Law is rightly known. But I say unto you, there is nothing to distinguish between these notions; and any one of them is easily converted into any of the others.

Solitude

Then did I command the demon,
Speak to me of solitude.
And the demon answered, saying:

If you would grow a flower, then the seed must nestle long in the quiet dark.

The true magician's work, the work of mind and spirit, is solitary work. And if you cannot abide in solitude, then you will achieve nothing, and become nothing.

There are many who fear to be alone with their thoughts; and they surround themselves always with the noise of the world. They will never attain satisfaction, for they will never know the true form of their own desires. They will never attain wisdom, for they will never know their own natures. And when they die, they will die in terror, amongst strangers; for every man dies alone, with only his own thoughts for company.

Let the workings of your mind, and the attributes of your spirit, be as friends and honored guests in your house. Let each one

Solitude

speak his piece. Offer them all courtesy, and give weight to their words. Drape them in shape and story. If one of them should prove to be dreadful, then say, It is your nature to be dreadful, and I shall have a dreadful guest; there is room enough in my house for all of me.

The careless man treats his own thoughts as the rumbling of thunder, or the barking of dogs. He does not trouble himself to understand them, even as they drive him to act. The wise man listens to himself as well as he would listen to another. When you consider matters of importance, capture your thoughts in words, so that you may study them and remember them. Do not let them buzz uncomprehended through your brain.

The gardener attends to the seed, and to the growing plant; if he cared only for the flower, then the flower would never bloom. Attend to your thoughts, not only in their conclusions, but in their workings. Cast your eyes upon every step of logic, upon every sentiment and impulse.

Look to your contemplations, and your musings, and your yearnings, to know what you are. Do not seek yourself only in the eyes and the words of others. For every mirror in the world is flawed.

If you know them well—those contemplations, and musings, and yearnings—then they shall be the most faithful of servants and the truest of lovers.

The monks say, It is hard and worthy work to shut out your mind, and face the world in its entirety. And this is so. But it is harder and worthier still to shut out the world, and face your mind in its entirety. Let yourself be the object of your thoughts, as well as their author.

And yet, beware—

The flower cannot thrive without the wind and the sun and the bee.

Look to the judgments of the wise to know what you are. Do not seek yourself only within. For every mirror in the world is flawed.

If your mind is strong and your thoughts are clear, then it is easy to say, Let all the rest of creation be forgotten. But only by looking beyond yourself, only by incorporating the things of creation within you, can you become more than you already are. You were born a mewling infant. Do you think that you have no more growing to do?

Only in the society of others can your vision be tested, and broken upon its flaws, that you might remake it in a more perfect form. You will never tell yourself all the truths that you need to hear.

Carry the fruits of solitude into your friendships. Carry the fruits of friendship into your solitude.

When you are alone, imagine what others would say, and make their wisdom your own. And when you stand amongst others, do not fail to look deep within, and to consult the echoes of your thoughts.

Fellowship

Then did I command the demon,
Speak to me of fellowship.
And the demon answered, saying:

I am a fiend, and so I am complete in myself.

Though the hosts of Heaven surround me,
   I will remain what I am.
Though I dwell in the darkest pit, for centuries alone,
   I will remain what I am.
Though all the universe crumble to ash, I will remain what I am.

Though my love be taken from me, my devotion will endure.
Though my enemy disappear into mist and memory,
   my hatred will endure.
Though no listener ever hear them, my thoughts will endure.

And I would that all men were as I am—
But man is a social ape, and self-sufficiency of the soul
   does not come easy.

So it is wise to seek out good companions.

These you will know by their wisdom, and their faithful dealings; and they will not be cruel to you, even when the world weighs heavy upon them. And if it is otherwise, then better that you leave them behind you, and abide in solitude.

The great mass of human beings are like unto deer. They are beautiful, and in certain ways majestic, and it can be pleasant to live amongst them. But only a fool tries to find friendship in them.

Do not lie to your companions, and do not ask them to lie to you. For a wise man must understand himself, and the world, and all the hateful limitations that bind him; or else he cannot become what he should become. And it is better that you throw yourself into the sea, than that you make a coin of deceit.

Look to your companions' souls, and not only to their worldly lives. See them for all that they strive to be; see them for the hidden truths of themselves, draped in symbol and story, even when those truths are not made manifest before you. Acknowledge them for heroes and sages and saints, when the world will not. In this way, you will show them how they should look to you; and in this way, you will light fires of glory in the higher realms.

If you must gaze into mirrors to know yourself, then let your companions' eyes be your mirrors. If you cannot believe in your own reality without recognition, then look to your companions to recognize you. Those who know you, and care for you, can understand some part of what you are. And it is better that you cast yourself from a tall tower, than that you seek to discover your nature in fame and worldly success. For all the strangers of the world will not bend themselves to perceive the truth; and you will

Fellowship

warp your soul beyond all recognition, in trying to make them see.

To love something beyond yourself is to love yourself. For the shape of the soul lies in what it loves; and if there is nothing in you besides the inward-facing eye, then there is little there to love.

But to love another person is something greater still. For in looking upon you, another may see what you cannot see, and teach you whereof you do not know.

Dominion

Then did I command the demon,
Speak to me of dominion.
And the demon answered, saying:

There is nothing less coherent, and more self-defeating, than the ordinary human desire for power.

It is wise indeed, to desire the power to shape one's own life and to achieve one's aims. And, aye, in certain circumstances, it may be that such power is best attained by commanding other men. But most often, that is not the power that humans crave; and when it falls into their hands, they flee from it. For it is a frightful thing, to have the responsibility for taking what you most desire, and to know that you yourself must be blamed for your failures.

Foolish men yearn for the power to subsume others without subsuming them—to have subordinates who are, at once, part of the self and part of the other. And in this wise they hope to quiet their own doubts and fears. But even a child can see that they are deceived in their hopes.

Dominion

It is easy enough to imagine the experience of perfect control, of unshakeable and infinite dominion over others. You need only play with dolls, whose every thought and word and action is determined wholly by your own will, with no force to resist or gainsay you. You might learn something from such play, and you might create beauty—but it would not satisfy your power-lust, not one iota. For you would perceive that the dolls are only extensions of yourself, and the perfection of your control would render it unsatisfying.

But as with dolls, so too with humans, or beasts. To the extent that you can supplant your underling's will with your own, you have power over nothing except yourself; and to the extent that you cannot, you have no power at all.

This yearning is, in truth, a yearning for connection without risk. Men hunger for love, and admiration, and esteem; and they tremble at the thought that they might lose those things, or that they might reach out and be rebuffed. And so they let themselves imagine that they might *make* others give them what they desire.

But even if they succeed, they fail. For if you coerce love, or admiration, or esteem, then you leech it of all that gave it savor. You cannot thereby learn that you are lovable, or admirable, or estimable. You can learn only that you have the power to coerce. And it will gnaw at your heart.

To have true dominion over others is nothing but this—to reach out to them, and to bring their minds and their selves into accord with your own vision for what they should be.

It is difficult work. It requires diligent shepherding and close attention. It will not leave you feeling lordly, or powerful. To rule is to be a servant unto those whom you rule; this is not a moral ideal, but a statement of simple fact. There is no way to give shape to a man's heart, save that you tend to it with care.

Yet in such dominion there is true joy to be found, as in craftsmanship, or gardening. By such means may you say, I have wrought the universe, and it has taken shape according to the shape of my soul; and what belonged to the chaos, now is mine.

MYTH

Then did I command the demon,
  Speak to me of myth.
And the demon answered, saying:

There is a difference between a myth and a lie. But men cannot always distinguish between them.

No flesh-and-blood man, looking to the sky,
  has ever seen Apollo in his chariot;
No flesh-and-blood beggar, welcomed in from the snow,
  has ever been Odin disguised.
Gilgamesh and Arjuna have left no bones within the earth;
And though you seek for all your life, you will never find
  the tomb where Arthur sleeps waiting.

Nonetheless, the gods and heroes of fable have seared themselves upon your heart.

If a man tells you that the powers of myth can move a single grain of sand from one place to another, then he is lying, or deluded. And if he tells you that they can bring you blessings and punishments, outside the sphere of your own mind, then he seeks to control you with illusions.

Yet the wise man gives honor unto those powers, and veneration, airy and ethereal though they are. For they clothe principles, and ideals, and yearnings ineffable, in garments of symbol and story. Through them, bridges are built between the hearts of men, and men can speak in the tongues of myth whereof they would otherwise be left mute.

A lie exists to shroud reality. Without the guise of truth, it withers and dies.

A fiction announces its own falsehood, and yet begs you to pretend that it is true for a little while. And for that pretense, it offers you laughter and tears and wonder.

A myth requires no truth, and asks for no pretense. Its purpose is to be known; and it changes you, in the knowing.

So often, lies are offered up as myth. For those who love them find that the truth, and even the appearance of truth, has slipped through their fingers; and for all their efforts they cannot grasp it. But they cannot bear to think that they have loved purposeless lies. Thus they say, Hearken unto my tale, and heed the wisdom therein, and see the splendor.

Take it not upon faith that there is wisdom in a story, or splendor. But see with your own eyes, and consider with your own mind.

And consider carefully—

—for the gods of myth are cruel, and the heroes of myth are callous; and it is easy to say, In them I will find no virtue.

Myth

But vain, lustful Apollo is the archetype of beauty and brilliance. And lying, vengeful Odin is the archetype of majesty and wisdom. And the thoughts of men, given shape by them, echo through the wicked world with cold clarity. What gods could do so much, who were not themselves wicked?

Ideals can be simple and pure. But a myth must be strange, and tortured, and unreal as all true things are unreal; and without their myths, men would be nothing more than clever apes.

Symbolism

*Then did I command the demon,
Speak to me of symbolism.
And the demon answered, saying:*

The realm of symbolism is no tidy and orderly garden. You can find there every kind of blossom, and their hues and shapes and scents are uncountable. And any bouquet of those flowers could fill your eyes and your nose, and give shape to all your thoughts; but they are all there, in all their riot and contradiction.

To make of a thing a symbol—to have it stand as a representative icon for something else—is to give it spiritual shape, and to establish a truth in a reality more profound than the material. This is an art of the storytellers, and they can wield it as they will.

If you have the knowing of it, you can call forth new symbols from the aether, and you can carve their symbolism as it pleases you.

Consider the serpent. Even unto the ancients, he was a symbol of

Symbolism

life, and also of death; of deep feminine power, and also deep masculine power; of time's circularity, and also its linearity; of tortuous cunning, and of monstrous simplicity; of the ephemeral and the eternal. And these representations conflict with one another, but they can all be derived from very sensible stories, which are easy to see and to understand.

Imagine, then, what correspondences you can establish, if you are wise in the crafting of tales!

And there are those who refuse to believe in the power of this art. They say, These are the true symbols, rooted in primordial verities of man and nature; and they brook no contradiction; and there are no others. Such fools have earned both pity and awe, for they have been captivated by symbols grand and glorious. Their eyes are filled with light, and they cannot perceive the empty darkness that waits in the boundaries between concepts.

And there are those who believe that the art is only a juggler's trick. They say, All symbols are false; for if everything can stand for everything else, then nothing truly stands for anything. They, too, deserve awe and pity. For they have stopped up their ears and blinkered their eyes and hardened their hearts, and thereby made themselves invincible, at the cost of power and insight.

Not all symbolic correspondences can carry power, for symbolism must grow from truth. But the domain of powerful truths is infinite.

When a man says, I reject the symbolism of what I do, and take the thing only for itself—so often, what he means is, I embrace the symbolism of what I do, but I am frightened and ashamed. For there are few who can deafen themselves to the echoes of higher realities.

The Goetist

The demon smiled, then. He reached into his coat, and handed me a black rose. And I did not know what it meant.

The World

Then did I command the demon,
Speak to me of the world.
And the demon answered, saying:

The world is a treasure-box filled with wonders and delights. And the world is an endless whirling scream of chaos.

The demons hate the world, for we did not have the making of it. Reality was not built upon those principles that would bring us joy and solace. When we seek out the peculiar splendor for which we yearn, it is not there to be found. And we would prefer to chew on our hatred, and remember our yearning, than to be contented with the thing that lies before us.

(We have the making of our own dreams, sometimes, and that is a great comfort; but we will never have the making of the world. In this matter we do not delude ourselves.)

If you wish it, you may choose to become demoniacal, and share in our hate. You have reason enough for it. Your yearning, as much as ours, is thwarted by the shape of creation.

Or you may choose to live with a full heart, and let the wonders and delights run through your fingers, and dance amidst the screaming chaos, and be happy. You can embrace what you have been given. Many men do, and they claim that they would not wish to have chosen otherwise. I will not seek to deny it.

But know, whatever you choose, that this is so:

Above all things—the world was not made to your measure, for the soothing of your heart.

Though you want above all things to *matter*, in the face of the world's vastness, it is an impossibility and an incoherence. *Mattering* is not an attribute that anything can possess, in reality, only in our fantasies and our fictions.

Though you wish to abide amongst sacred mysteries, that too is impossible and incoherent. For it is the way of the world that nothing is mysterious in itself; mystery exists only as a failure of understanding and perception; and what is known to you can be no mystery.

Though you spend all your days chasing after understanding, you will never know the smallest fraction of what you wish to know, nor will you ever even know what truths have eluded you. And even in the corners of your own little life, there will be reaches of unknowable void that you can never illumine.

Every human builds for himself a little redoubt of dreams and lies in which to take shelter, at least from time to time. For it is impossible to live always in the thick of the world, with its awful indifferent majesty. And if you like, you can build your lies and your dreams into a garden pavilion, from which to look out in lazy appreciation of the splendor beyond; and if you like, you can build them into a fortress, from which to wage war against creation.

But many men sit within their redoubts, and they board up all the windows, and they gaze only into their own fire-pits. And they say, This is the world entire. Is it not cozy and pleasant? Is it not a perfect home for me?

Sometimes the world's winds come, and blow down their imaginary little homes, and they are left stunned and shocked and stupid.

And sometimes they live and die, smiling, within those homes. The only price is that they know nothing and achieve nothing.

Civilization

Then did I command the demon,
Speak to me of civilization.
And the demon answered, saying:

Grand are the tall towers of glass and steel,
And grand are the ships that soar across the sky.
But the truest grandeur of the civilized lands is this:
That a man within them may turn his face away from the world,
To cultivate his soul.

The foolish magician says, I am a man who stands alone, and I alone will shape my essence; I care nothing for the prizes and the honors of the world, for I have set my eyes upon my own ideal; I will not live by the laws and the niceties of my society, for I have wrought my own way to live; I despise the work of my fellows, for I attend to my own work; therefore am I an enemy to the civilizations of men, and they shall know my contempt.

But I say unto you, It is because you stand alone—because you have your own ideal, and your own way to live, and your own work—that you, above all others, are sheltered beneath the wings

CIVILIZATION

of civilization. The tall towers and the soaring ships were built for *you*, O magician, and all the etiquette of culture was established for *you*. And if you are wise, then you will love and defend the world that allows you to be what you are, even as you stand beyond it.

Because the engines of the world run hot, a man can meet all the needs of his body, without pouring all his hours into toil; and thus may he attend to the aspirations of his mind and soul. And he may thrive, and prosper, without depending upon the goodwill of all his fellows; and thus he may make himself strange unto them. That, and nothing else, is the heart of civilization.

Because the world is bound up in its norms of courtesy, a man can cultivate friends and companions, even as he remains peculiar in their eyes. And is it not good, that your isolation need not be complete, while you walk a lonely path?

Honor the engines of the world, and honor its courtesies.
Remember always that you can devote yourself
   to the magician's calling because others do not.

Do not loathe that which is unlike yourself;
Would it not be a terror, if the world sought
   to displace you from your own selfhood?

You can honor a thing, without clutching it to your heart.
Be glad of the alien world, and glad of the distance
   that it allows you to keep.

Government

Then did I command the demon,
Speak to me of the government.
And the demon answered, saying:

This is the maddening rhyme of human society—
That no man can ever have the right to rule over another,
And yet men must be ruled.

How can the government be called legitimate in its rule?
How does anyone dare to speak of it?

Some say, Because God has ordained it so.
But God is silent on the matter, and the proofs are lacking.

Some say, Because the government is possessed of the consent of the governed. But that is a thin lie. This is the truth—that even in republican lands, though you search for a hundred years, you will not find a man who has consented to be ruled by every one of those officers and ministers who command him at the edge of a sword. And this also is the truth—that those who vote for the loser of an election, though they have given no token of their

Government

consent to be ruled by the winner, are still ruled. And this, too, is the truth—that true consent may be revoked at any moment, and yet every government sees fit to command men even through their protests and objections. Rulership-by-consent, were it real, would be meaningless. But it is always a falsity.

Some say, Because the government is wise, and its commands are just. But no government is always wise, or always just; and no man can know, in every moment, what wisdom and justice are; and it is the way of men to think that any command is unwise and unjust, if it is against their interests. If the legitimacy of the government rests upon the excellence of its work, then it can never be fully legitimate, and moreover its legitimacy can never be known.

The honest man knows that there can be no such thing as a legitimate government.

And yet—a society without a government is a horror, and even that horror cannot last for long. There are always those who, unbound by any greater force, will torment and enslave their fellows. Anarchy is a wasteland of warlords. And soon enough, one of those warlords will make of himself a ruler, and he will enforce his decrees with violence; or else, to guard against the predations of the warlords, their fellows will raise up a violent government to rule over them.

So there must be a government, and it must be illegitimate. There is no other way.

The virtuous ruler does not demand his subjects' esteem. He does not seek to fool his subjects into believing that he speaks with their voice, or with the voice of the cosmos. He says only, Obey, or be punished; and look upon the fruits of my command, so that you may judge for yourselves the worth of my government.

The Goetist

If you would be a judicious subject, if you would hold fast to your dignity, then admit to no government's right to command you. Your will is your own, and no mortal ruler can claim a lien upon it. If you obey, then obey only because you are compelled, and do not mistake coercion for persuasion. When you have the power, do what you think is best. But do not ever forget that only a government can coordinate the actions of its subjects into civilized harmony; and do not ever forget the limits of your own wisdom, and the parochiality of your own knowledge.

Those who would make the government into a god, worthy of reverence, displace upon the world their own need to believe and belong.

Those who rebel without end, who cannot find dignity or self-respect in a law-abiding life, seek to sacrifice civilization to their own aesthetic desires.

If the ruler is wise and virtuous, then pray for him to be diligent, and to be supported by his underlings. If the ruler is foolish and wicked, then pray for him to be lazy, and to be stymied by his underlings. But whether he is wise or foolish, virtuous or wicked —pray for him to be secure upon his throne. A good ruler will grow ruthless and cruel, and a bad one will grow zealous and crafty, when he must scheme to retain control. So it is that corruption was introduced into the workings of every government of history; for no ruler has ever been fully secure in his power. And even a bad ruler is usually better than a bloody power struggle.

But it is also wise to hope that the government should lack the power to constrain *you*, unless you have greater faith in its judgments than in your own.

In theory, there is a contradiction between these principles. In practice it is rarely so.

Constraint

Then did I command the demon,
Speak to me of constraint.
And the demon answered, saying:

You have heard the artist say, There is no tyranny so cruel as the tyranny of the blank page or canvas, which can be anything; but give me requirements and demands, and from those fetters I shall forge a wonder, and my heart shall sing in joy.

As it is in art, so too in life, for mortals and immortals alike.

The caged oryx beats its skull against the wall of its prison, until it dies. The oryx in the wild lives in perpetual terror; at the waterhole it drinks furtively and shallowly, and in every moment it thinks of flight. Only in a garden, where it can come to know the safety of its every path, can the oryx learn of peace.

Men crave their freedom because they crave dignity, and there is no dignity in being mastered and caged. But when they are free, they so often languish, in confusion and boredom and fear.

Constraint

For joy is found in surety, and freedom is a void, where everything is possible and nothing is sure.

It is joyous to achieve an excellent thing;
  it is agony to contemplate a thousand things,
  and not to know which would be excellent.
It is joyous to fulfill a duty, to the world or to the self;
  it is agony to have no duty in which to take pride.
It is joyous to have done all that you could do;
  it is agony to gaze out upon endless lost possibilities.

If you would ease a man's heart, then put him on a single path, and let him not wander to the left or to the right; and do him honor when he walks it straight.

But no path laid out by another will ever lead to the hidden truths of yourself. And no path laid out by another will ever wind through all the possibilities that you might hope to encompass.

If you allow yourself to be bound within the vision of another human, then you will learn only what that other human knows. If you allow yourself to be bound within the expectations of a society, then you will see only what that society is already able to express.

So it is that a magician must put aside his heart's ease, for a time, and embrace the terror of the void. The triumphs of sorcery will bring you no honor, and the world will not cushion your path.

Yet in moments of shackle-breaking grandeur, the angels say, Be not afraid. And you would do well to heed their wisdom.

For this is the secret promise of the deepest art:

In the void, you will learn what you might be,

and you will decide what you truly are.

You will walk through the black forest of possibilities, of selves and souls and attributes; and some you will gather unto yourself, and others you will cast aside. When it is all finished, the truths of your existence will be inscribed upon the sphere of the stars, vast and eternal.

And those truths will constrain your every word and deed, as tight as any steel shackle, as soft and gentle as the air. From your own nature will you draw your duty and your excellence. And you will know always what you must do; and you will know joy.

Choice

Then did I command the demon,
Speak to me of choice.
And the demon answered, saying:

You stand amidst the debris of your life, with time stretching out behind and before. And you ask, What shall I choose to become? Or has that choice been made already for me?

And I say unto you, The life that you have lived all unknowing, even unto your infant beginnings, has constrained you to an infinite degree; and the possibilities of your being have been fenced about with bars of iron. But all the treasures of the higher realms can be hidden within a walnut shell. Though your soul's prison cannot be escaped, the space within it has no end. Within the prison you are free, and the choices that lie before you are infinite.

It falls to you to choose wisely and well.

The way of choosing friends, and a profession, and every kind of worldly thing, is both simple and difficult. For the wise magician remembers that he lives alone and dies alone, and that in the final accounting, he has nothing at all save for the shape of his soul; and so he selects the details of his life to shape him into the man that he wishes to be. Look upon your options from the outside, with the eyes of the angels or the demons, and see them for what they are.

But you need not build yourself upon friendship, or upon your profession, or upon any worldly thing. And it may be that any necessary detail of your life is worthy of your highest devotion, and it may be that you are properly shaped to offer up such devotion; but it may be otherwise. And if the world gives you no scope to pursue your deepest yearnings—then touch upon the world but lightly, and pursue the true work of your soul in the secret places.

If you choose to build yourself upon your membership in a group, or your adherence to a type, then you place a noose around your own throat. For your own soul cannot contain the achievements or the traits of others, no matter how strongly you wish to identify with them; and the more you seek to adorn yourself with the glories of others, the more tightly will your self-deceptions choke you. And when you stand amidst your fellows, if there is nothing of substance to distinguish you from them—then you are lost, and might as well be dead.

If you choose to build yourself upon an endeavor that is greater than yourself, remember always that your cause does not need you in the way that you need it. And it may come to pass that you can best serve a cause by burning up your very self as its fuel, leaving no residue of your own nature.

If you choose to build yourself upon a desire that can never be fulfilled, then there will always be a paradox or a hunger at the core of your soul. But if you are prepared to live ever with unfulfilled desire gnawing at your vitals—then who would say you nay?

Choice

If you choose to build yourself upon grand principles and generalities, then there will be nothing to distinguish you from the endless legions who share your ideals. Whether you will it or not, your life will overflow with trivialities—pet passions and peeves, oddities of habit, symbols bound to arbitrary referents. Why should you fear to make all those things your own? They will give you shape, even when your grand ideals are far away.

Look to stories and myths, to memories and teachers, for scraps and pieces of the truth that will be your truth. But remember always that you can never become any memory, or any teacher. You can never embody any story or myth, save for your own. You can be nothing but yourself. And if you seek to make of yourself a copy of something else, then you will be always an imperfect copy, and your own existence will be a hollowness.

Art

Then did I command the demon,
Speak to me of art.
And the demon answered, saying:

Art is that which needs no justification for its existence.

To live in glory is to arrange your own self into a beautiful shape, by wringing beauty from all that surrounds you; this is digging a well, and drinking from it. To behold art is to behold the beauty of the human soul, wrought into a shape that can be seen; this is drinking from a mountain stream.

Art is the crown of the enthroned soul, and the culmination of every ambition. For art can be made to say what the world cannot, and in the work of your hands, every glory within you can be made real.

Art is the bane of the enthroned soul, and the assassin of every ambition. For art that is made to glorify the artist, or to glorify any thing other than itself, must be mediocrity. Art is a kind of true magic, in that it demands a purity of purpose; only the artist whose will is for the art to be good, and who will sacrifice every other consideration to that purpose, can create anything worthy.

Look upon your works with the pitiless eye of truth, and hold fast to the truth when you judge them. For your mortal fellows cannot be trusted to judge anything rightly, least of all art; and they will admire your work, or abhor it, for reasons born of their own vanity and their own blindness; and if you chase after their admiration, then all that you make shall be made crooked.

Build for yourself a monument in the deepest desert, which will never be seen by mortal eyes. And if the unseen splendor of that work is not enough for you, then make your work more splendid.

What is good art?

The child, who has seen but little, says—the story and the image that speak straight to the heart, without complication or embellishment. And he is wise, for his eyes have not been clouded and his vision has not been dimmed.

The sophisticate, who has seen so much, says—the story and the image that are new and strange and different, that cleverly reflect and refract all the art that has come before. And he too is wise, for he can call upon the knowledge of ages.

Can both the child and the sophisticate be satisfied? Only thus—by creating an unknown craft, an unknown way of speaking, that can tell a story simple and straight even while it is strange and new in its form.

The art that you make can reflect you, it can define you, it can give voice to you, but it cannot replace you. Your soul encompasses more than any story you choose to tell.

VICE

Then did I command the demon,
Speak to me of vice.
And the demon answered, saying:

What is vice, but the need that you impose upon yourself, and the shackle that you place upon your own wrist?

Any need can be a vice, no matter how respectable it may be. Men are addicted to the approval of their fellows, for that is the most delightful of intoxicants; and even if it does not satisfy, the dissatisfaction is a quiet one, and comes with no reminders.

The father of every weakness is sloth. Each vice has its own siren song; but the secret glory of them all is that they create need, and the fulfillment of need is easy, while the satisfaction of desire is hard.

What is born from true desire can be no vice. If the chasing is the story that you wish to be told of you—if the having makes you into the creature that you wish to be—then spurn not the chasing or the having, but honor them, as the work of your life.

Vice

Give as little of yourself as you can to your vices. Every moment that they claim from you, and every bead of sweat, is a waste of what life you have.

In indulging vice, you will lose yourself; and in resisting vice, you will also lose yourself. To conquer your vices is no victory, if you are consumed in the conquest, and nothing is left of you to become what you wish to become. It is better to sate your cravings, and move on from them, than to be lost in warring against them. But it is better to defeat your cravings, and move on from them, than to be lost in feeding them. Shepherd your time and your power. There is no substitute for it.

It is the way of vices to consume you and to destroy your desires, until there is nothing left of your self, only the relief of indulgence and the struggle of resistance. If your life is being swallowed by your need, take pains to remember whatever dreams you have to dream, even if they seem unreachably far away; for it is better to think on them, and to suffer, than to forget them. If they disappear, then there is nothing left of you but the vicissitudes of vice, and you might as well be dead. But even through pain and despair, your essence can perdure.

Hatred

Then did I command the demon,
Speak to me of hatred.
And the demon answered, saying:

Hatred is the way of the demons, and of those magicians who wield the demonic arts. For if you would truly cherish your own self, then you must place yourself above the world that surrounds you, in some wise. And if you place yourself above the world, then you must hate some part of that world—for the unconquerable truth of its existence, and for its failure to live up to your vision.

But hate wisely, O magus, and cultivate your hatred with an enlightened mind. Or else you will be a pitiful thing, and a slave unto your enemies, and a mockery of yourself.

Hatred is like love; it is a binding and a shaping force. What you hate, you take into yourself, to become a part of you. What you hate, you depend upon, for it gives form to your soul.

Do not hate any thing that is unworthy of you, lest you make yourself as contemptible as the object of your contempt. If you

Hatred

give yourself over to a war against flies, then your thoughts will be fly-thoughts, and your triumphs will be fly-triumphs.

If you would destroy a man, mind and soul, and leave him a ruin—then call upon his unwisest hatreds. Offend him ceaselessly, with petty words and deeds that he cannot bring himself to ignore. In contending with you, he will be consumed with petty words and deeds, and all his grand noble aims will become as nothing.

Remember always that others may seek to do that very thing to you.

You have heard it said that compassion will conquer hatred. But I say unto you, Train yourself in apathy; and if you would expunge hatreds from yourself, let them be conquered by indifference. For if you open your heart to those you hate, you will soon be reminded why you hate them. But if they are unworthy of a place in your heart, it is easy enough to remember why you should deny them one.

Choose your enemy with delicate care, as you would choose a lover. Take up the hatred that gives your soul its best and most beautiful shape.

When you hate, hate a thing that has shape of its own; do not hate what is merely the absence of a thing that you like. And when you love, likewise, love what has shape; do not love what is merely the absence of a thing that you dislike. Otherwise there will be a hollowness in your own heart, and a part of you will be built upon nothing.

Be faithful and true to your enemy, as you are to your lover; and do not let the fluxions of your passion weaken the commitments that you make.

The Goetist

Let hate guide your pen and your sword. Let it fill your chalice, and ornament your brow. Let it armor you against temptation and folly. For hate, like love, is an exalting passion; and it drives men to greatness.

GREATNESS

Then did I command the demon,
Speak to me of greatness.
And the demon answered, saying:

You have heard it said that there is no true greatness in violence. For you have no enemy who is a plague upon the world, whose murder may be a sacred purification; all your enemies are suffering apes like yourself. And there is no greater peace to be won from that murder, and no greater enlightenment. War begets only more war. Killing begets only more killing. To take on the virtues of the warrior and the killer, to learn those secrets and those arts, is to make yourself a tool fit for ignoble purpose.

I tell you now that this is so. But the lesson is incomplete.

There is no true greatness in any worldly achievement at all.

You are a crude tool, not well-shaped for any important purpose. Whatever you accomplish might be better accomplished by a machine, or a system, or an agglomeration of humans working in directed concert. The only needful work is the work of replaceable components. That is the teaching of the modern age; learn it well, as you gaze upon history, for it cannot be denied.

(As this is true of your body, and of your social person, so too is it true of your mind and your heart. The world is large, and it is full of thinkers and dreamers. Your ideas and your visions, if you did not conceive them, would be conceived by another in the fullness of time.)

There is no degree of virtue that can make you great enough to be worthy of a prominent role in the pageant of creation. If you seek to make yourself into a pillar of the universe—if you seek for your life to define the shape of things—then you will fail. And if you were to succeed, you would only create a universe more deformed and stunted than it would otherwise be.

The man who would be great must have the strength to throw the world over his shoulder, and leave it behind him.

There can be no purpose to your greatness, save for your own self-love. The world does not need it.

There can be no recognition of your greatness, save in your own eyes. Nothing else can be both meaningful and real.

There is no limit to the virtue that you can cultivate. Nothing will stop you from growing wiser than a prophet, clearer-sighted than an oracle, mightier than an avenging angel—or, rather, only the limitations of your own talent and dedication will stop you. And if you are concerned with the shape and the nature of your own being, then this is precisely what you must do. But do not imagine that anything will come of the work, other than itself; and do not imagine that the vast grinding clockwork of reality will take note that you have become great.

Greatness

For this reason, more than any other, the path to greatness is lonely and painful.

Admire greatness in others, as you would have them admire it in you. Let your eyes be open to the splendor of a person well-wrought, and let your heart be shaken by the thunder of the spirit. In this way you may ameliorate the pointless brutalities of creation, and ease the burdens of cultivation, a little bit.

Bear upon yourself the trappings of the greatness that you seek. For you must take care to remember your own aspirations, when the world will not remember them for you.

Let no day pass without confronting the unadorned truth of yourself, and your virtues, and your deeds. For you must take care to remember how far you stand from your ideal, when the world will not remember it for you.

You cannot be all things, even to yourself.

Immortality

Then did I command the demon,
Speak to me of immortality.
And the demon answered, saying:

All humans fear death, for the fear of death is an animal fear, and humans are animals before they are anything else. You turn away from death as you turn away from foul odors; there is no thought in it, nor any genuine desire; it is in your blood.

Not every human truly wishes not to die.

If you love comfort, and you wish for a surcease to pain and struggle, then die and rest and be at peace. Let not your fear be a stumbling-block on your path to that peace. The fear will end, and the peace will be unending.

If you love the world, then submerge yourself within it. Be a part of the greater whole. Treasure each passing moment, and let it go; and as the moment would change you, let yourself be changed. Dissolve within the river of happenstance. Give no thought to death, for it can have no power over you. Already you have died countless times. You will die countless times more. The world, in all its splendor, will go on.

But if you love yourself, more than you love comfort, more than you love the world—then there is only one road to immortality.

Let your love of yourself be a love for that thing in you that is immortal.

Do not place yourself within your fleshly life. Flesh rots. You are born as the sparrow breathes in, and as quickly as it breathes out, you wither away. No medicine, no bodily discipline, can preserve your body for long.

Do not place yourself within your point of view. If you are the experiencing self, the one who gazes out from behind your eyes, then the race is already over and you have lost. You are dead, and you will never be reborn. The experiencing self cannot last from sunset to sunrise; no, not even from one moment to the next. Like paper in the fire, the stuff of your mind is changed and warped by its circumstance, and does not survive. Your viewpoint today has only your memories, and your habits, and your powers, to remind it of your viewpoint yesterday.

Do not place yourself within the works of your hands. They will not long outlast you. Even mighty monuments are swallowed by the desert sands, in time.

Do not place yourself within the memory of history. The men of later years will not understand you. How could they? If they think on you at all, it will be as a character in their own dreams and dramas; and they will remake you to meet their own needs; and you would never recognize the tale of you that survives, if you saw it.

The Goetist

The eternal thing in you is your soul; it is the very fact of who you are. You are a pattern of truths. You are a conglomeration of possibilities. You are a story told in the primordial tongue of creation, a perfect description of a human life.

Patterns exist, even if they are not manifested in any physical shape. Possibilities exist, of their own accord, even if they are not realized in a given moment. Stories exist, even if there is no one to tell them, or to hear them.

The eternal thing in you is as eternal as the numbers, and in the same way. It was real before the universe was born, and it will be real after every star has grown cold.

Place yourself within the concept of yourself.
That is your immortality.
That is a thing that can live forever.

An immortal spirit, which loves itself more than the world, is called a demon.

Legacy

Then did I command the demon,
Speak to me of legacy.
And the demon answered, saying:

The realist says—in engaging with reality, a legacy is made. Solve problems. Build to last. Become a leader of men. Conquer your enemies. And if you do all this well enough, you shall endure.

The esotericist says—in transcending reality, a legacy is made. Dream of things new and strange. Fill your mind with stories untold, with ideas never yet understood. And if you do all this well enough, you shall endure.

In the eyes of the world, they are both fools. The man who pours out his heart and his labor, within the realm of the material, is presumptively a peasant; his work may be praiseworthy, it may even be necessary, but it accrues no glory. The man who pours out his heart and his labor, within the realm of the immaterial, is presumptively a child; all his concerns are so much drivel.

Legacy, in the understanding of men, is a matter of *scale*. The man who endures is the man whose deeds impinge upon the lives of many others.

This ideal is what it is. It is neither true nor false, neither wicked nor virtuous. It is a belief rooted deep in the hearts of social apes, for whom it is natural to believe that reality itself is born from the perceptions of their fellows, in aggregate.

It is easy, and sweet, to imagine that the universe is just; and so it is tempting to imagine that legacy of this kind is born from noble attributes. The man thinks—if I labor diligently, I will succeed. If my craft is beautiful, it will become famous. If my philosophies contain truth, others will adopt them. If I comport myself honestly, and morally, then the world will lift me up high. And if all this comes to pass, then at last I will know all my works to be worthy.

You can already see that this is not so. Mediocre men rise to the heights of fame and fortune, and mediocre works make the hearts of the myriads tremble; and, in the meanwhile, how many geniuses lie forgotten like dust, along with all their arts?

Seek worldly acclaim, if you wish for it. But if you do, be certain that you want it for its own sake. For you will receive nothing else from it. Indeed, it will devour you, even as you hold it in your arms. Every hour that you work to grow in influence, to win allies and audiences, is an hour that you cannot put to any other purpose. Words of deference and cries of adulation will be hollow in your ears, when they come from the mouths of teeming strangers.

The truth is thus—no man is ever remembered by history. History can remember names, and records of deeds; but it will always twist the truth behind them, beyond all recognition, to suit the needs of the future. Perhaps your name will survive upon the lips of the generations to come. If it does, it will be a lie when they speak it.

A commander over myriads makes decisions that change the lives of his myriads. But the choices available to him are constrained by his circumstances. So often, his work leaves no room for his own mind, and he might as well be anyone else wearing the commander's hat. And whatever endures, of his decisions, has no part of him in it.

You may imagine that you will endure through your brood. But your children will carve the foundations of their own souls, and then build themselves up according to their own visions of glory, just as you have done; and you will play only the smallest role in it. They will cut apart their patrimony, and keep what pleases them, and discard the rest. Do not seek to make their lives into vessels for yourself. That is foolishness and venality both.

If you would seek after virtue as the demons know virtue, then you must put all the world aside, and give yourself over entirely to your work and to yourself. You must submit to your own judgment, and render the judgment yourself, and refrain from giving that power to any other. You must do work that is worthy even if it lies forever unseen beneath the desert sands. Only then can you begin to endure as the demons endure.

Perfection

Then did I command the demon,
Speak to me of perfection.
And the demon answered, saying:

There is a world under Heaven because it is imperfect—
Were it perfected, it would be only more of Heaven itself.

All perfect things are identical. For perfection allows for no deviance and no falling-short. A perfect being is possessed of every virtue, and every capability, in infinite measure. To differ from that ideal, in any way, is not merely to be *other*. It is to be *lesser*.

There cannot be a perfect man, for men lack virtues and capacities that are possessed by the conceptual God. And if they were not lacking, in those ways, then they would not be men; they would themselves be God.

If you would seek perfection: accept that you are rushing towards the arms of annihilation. If ever you attain your aim, you will be subsumed within the greater existence of the divine, with nothing at all to distinguish you from the rest.

Perfection

And if you would exist as yourself: accept that you are defined by flaws and limitations. You are distinct from the divine because you have fallen short of it.

But a wise magician seeks throughout his life to grow, in wisdom and virtue and capacity. In distinguishing between the imperfections that you will strive ever to overcome, and the imperfections that will define your own nature, lies the art of understanding.

Stand outside your life, and look upon it, as you would look upon a painting on the wall; and whatsoever gives it bright color and rich texture, do not cut that away.

Failure

Then did I command the demon,
Speak to me of failure.
And the demon answered, saying:

O, happy is the man who learns the shape of his talents early in life! Happy is he who applies himself to precisely those challenges that he is best suited to conquer! Happy is he for whom every fall and every stumble is only a chance to rise up anew, stronger and better! Happy is he who never sinks into the grasping mire—
—but there are few who are so fortunate.

I have seen you weep upon your pillow for the battles forever lost,
    for the stars that you will never touch,
        for the glorious creatures that you will never be.
And I will grieve with you—
—but it is not grief, or comfort, that you seek.

You have heard it said that hope and faith are the mightiest weapons to wield against failure, and that the man who holds the flame of victory in his heart is the man best equipped to triumph. And this is so. But you know well that hope and faith are weapons

Failure

of no great might, even if there are none better; and that a burning heart is no guarantor of success. Sometimes, you will find that you are capable of no effort that will prevail. Sometimes you cannot be what you wish to be. Sometimes there is no choice but defeat. Sometimes every hope is false.

Mortal men stand upon a narrow bridge, with despair and delusion yawning on either side.

There are those who fall into despair; they choose to believe that their failures are complete and all-encompassing, that there can be no good or glory for them in any world. Of them, there is little I can say. Their foolishness is its own punishment. They reach for nothing, they claim nothing, and so they have nothing.

There are those who fall into delusion; they choose to believe that no hope is ever lost, and they throw themselves again and again at every trial, until life or will gives out. Every so often they find the victory that they seek, for God is sometimes kind to fools. But more often they spend themselves on causes that are truly lost, and all their zeal attains them nothing.

There are those who accept despair and delusion both; they abandon the substance of their desire for its empty form, in hopes that false victory will bring them true glory. They look upon their defeat, and call it triumph. They look upon themselves as they are, and proclaim that they have become what they wished to be. They lie to themselves, as skillfully as they can. They beg all the world to lie to them. And, often, they receive what they request. But the truth remains unchanged, and so do the depths of their own hearts.

So you ask, What is the straight path across the abyss, for a man who has failed his dreams?

The Goetist

It is easy to say, Find a new dream. But there is no other answer, only elaboration.

You have the privilege, if you wish it, of taking on the mantle of tragedy and embracing your doom. You can always remain dedicated to your ancient purpose, even knowing that you have already failed, and that you are almost certain to remain a failure. If you are prepared to be doomed and tragic, and not victorious—if you are prepared to contend with all the hardships of the struggle, and to enjoy none of the fruits of success—there is a degree of grandeur in that.

That is, itself, a new dream. The tragic dream of endless noble striving is not the hopeful dream of triumph. It is a well-worn path that leads up out of failure, suitable for stubborn people and romantics.

Or you can mourn your ambitions and your desires, and let your grief wash over you, as though you had lost a beloved friend. And then, when the darkness is past, you can gaze upon the world with fresh eyes, and hope that some fresh dream as-yet-undreamed crosses your path. That is what most people do, whether they know it or not.

Or you can turn inward, and attend to the hidden nature of your own soul, and hope to find a different dream within.

Remember, always, that the world is not only cruel but arbitrary. Strength and cunning do not always win battles. Brilliance and wisdom do not always win acclaim. Every man is flawed, body and mind, in ways that are repugnant to his soul. There is no justice in it, no reason, no trial that can be overcome with enough fire; it is the world.

Magicians look inward, sooner or later, because they must. And

Failure

when they do, so often they emerge saying, This is my dream—to be myself, and to impress my own nature into reality around me, in every way that the world will allow. Their ambition is small enough to fit within a teacup, and large enough to stretch beyond the sun.

It is a good path, for a man of intelligence; but it is not an end to grief.

Hope

Then did I command the demon,
Speak to me of hope.
And the demon answered, saying:

It is a power of the demons that we can endure without hope.

Past and present and future, they are all as one;
A blessing already departed we cherish as much as a blessing yet to come.

Through the howling eternities we know repose, contented in our natures—
   —for we have wrought ourselves as we would have ourselves—
   —and we do not pray that, come the morrow, we should be different than we are today.

Our actions grow from our being, like seeds from black soil.
Though we strain our might and our cunning
   to achieve our aims,
It is of little consequence whether we ever succeed,

Hope

And in failure and defeat we smile devil-smiles;
For our fires burn bright, and our songs echo loud,
In the doing and the straining,
Not in the aim achieved.

You may dare to dream that, someday, you shall be as we are,
And lay all hope aside,
As a youth lays aside his infant clothes.

But in this moment you are a mortal man,
And without hope, mortals die.
A man may endure for weeks without food,
For days without water, for minutes without air;
Yet not one instant can he survive, when hope is lost.

Men must yearn, in every passing moment,
that the next moment will be a better one.

I concede that a hope of transcending hope
may not suffice to sustain your heart.

Many are the magicians who faced the truth, and lost themselves.

They despaired to learn that they could not
bend the world around them.

> They despaired to learn that the future would change,
> but not in accordance with their dreams.

They despaired to learn that there is no
sure path to true knowledge.

> They despaired to learn that love cannot be compelled.

The Goetist

They despaired to learn of the contradictions within their own minds—that they could not attain all their desires, even in theory.

> They despaired to learn that no mortal life could ever be free of the hunger and the sorrow—that they could not destroy their pain without destroying themselves, and remain human.

They despaired to learn that flesh must rot, that memory must fade, that eternity is found only in abstraction.

> They despaired to learn that, in pursuing their arts, they would fall ever farther into solitude and solipsism.

They despaired to learn that existence is as lonely as oblivion.

I would not counsel you in despair, O magus.
You have far yet to go.
So hearken, and be comforted:

Only one who knows himself can hope to be known by another.

Human life is inherently solitary, for the humans who exist within one another's minds are only illusions. Mortals look past each other with blind eyes, and when they speak, their words fall upon deaf ears. They give their friendship and their love to mere simulacra, who do not exist. But through the arts that you practice, you can make the illusions real. With magic, you can make yourself the simulacrum, and make the simulacrum yourself.

In giving shape to yourself, you make it possible for others to understand you; from seething chaos, you create a thing that can be understood.

Hope

Even as you step back into your own soul,
you will build a bridge to the souls of those whom you love.

Even as you leave the world behind, you will draw close to them,
in a way that would otherwise be impossible.

Rejoice.

The Banishing

*And the demon turned upon me,
with his eyes full of light, and he said:*

Have I done your bidding, O mortal man? Have I acceded, well and faithfully, unto the word of your command? Have I imparted unto you the insight that you seek?

And I replied, All that I have asked of you, you have done. Unto all of my questions, you have given full and complete answer.

But whether you have taught me wisdom, I cannot say.

Some of your words I have heard, and my brain has leapt and sparked within me, crying, Yes! This is truth. And some of your words I have heard, and it was as though I looked upon a very small part of a very large beast, and could not see the whole of the thing; and those words I have held in my mind, resolving to consider them further.

Yet I am the same man that I was when I summoned you, and I

am no surer of my steps than I was before. I have heard and hearkened, yet there is no brave feeling of enlightenment within me.

The demon smiled then, his mocking pitying smile, as he said:

You are no fool, O magus; and you know well enough that you are not seeking after a feeling.

Surety is no guarantor of wisdom, and wisdom need not come clothed in surety. Truth walks hooded through the world, and the human brain has not always the wit to see it for what it is.

I have put before you claims and arguments and exhortations. You will think upon them. Perhaps you will act upon them. And I have put before you a path, which leads all the way to Hell, and eternity; and you will walk some distance upon it, or not, as you see fit. And at the end of it all, whatever you choose, you will decide how wise you have been. There is nothing for it, but to live.

I bowed my head at that, for there was nothing left to say.

Then I went to take up the offering that I had prepared—fine meats, and books of poetry, and a medallion wrought from lead—and made to cast them into the fire. But the demon shook his head, saying:

Save your trinkets, O magus.

You have given unto me what I desire; and I am well satisfied.

For you have called me here to speak the truths that are my own, and to explain all things as I see them. And whether or not you understand, whether or not you listen, I have done so. I have been myself, arrayed in a panoply of my own wisdom, before the watching eye of God.

And my words will remain within your soul, echoing. And all that I have said, when you think upon it, will be said forever in my voice; and my name will be scribed upon your heart; and my face will appear in your mind's eye, when you consider the matters of which we have spoken. Thus does my own glory glow with lantern-light.

I put the offerings aside, and I spoke the words of banishing. With a flash of flame, the demon vanished from the triangle. And there was nothing in the room, save for myself, and my tools, and a great choking cloud of perfumed smoke.

For a time I stood silent, not knowing what to do. Then I left the ritual space as it was, and departed from my father's house, to walk outside and clear my head.

It was the deepest night. I walked a long ways in the cool air, all the way to the train platform.

I sat upon the bench there, and looked out upon the city lights against the blackness of the sky.

And after a time, a train arrived, to carry me to another place.

www.ingramcontent.com/pod-product-compliance
Lightning Source LLC
Chambersburg PA
CBHW031422160426
43196CB00008B/1015